Unleash the Magic!

Unleash the Magic!

Winning Writings
from
the 2009
Hill Country Book Festival

Ann Bell, Editor

Assistant Editors - Susan Davidson,
Phyllis Moses, and Lynn Whitson

Katy Crossing Press

Unleash the Magic! Winners of the 2009 Hill Country Book Festival Writing Competition

Reproduction or translation of any part of this work beyond that permitted by section 107 or 108 of the 1976 United States Copyright Act without the permission of the copyright owner is unlawful. Request for permission or further information should be addressed to Hill Country Book Festival, Inc. http://www.hillcountrybookfestival.org by contacting:

Phyllis Moses, President phylmoses@msn.com or
Ann Bell, Vice-President annamaebell@suddenlink.net.

Katy Crossing Press
300 Katy Crossing
Georgetown, TX 78626

ISBN: 1-45054-915-2
ISBN-13: 978-1-45054-915-8

Dedication

To

Phyllis Moses

Whose dedication to literature and literacy is exemplary.

As a founding member of the Hill Country Book Festival, Inc., she has shown her leadership through continual service on the executive board and her tireless community support.

Hill Country Book Festival, Inc., (Georgetown, TX) organized in 2007 as a 501(c)3 non-profit agency, offers ways and means of enhancing the writing skills of local authors, raises levels of literacy in Central Texas and provides an affordable venue for writers to showcase their works. The organization is non-political and non-religious by its legal definition. HCBF works with local public and school libraries to supplement their reading and writing programs.

Table of Contents

Part I: Youth Division (Grades 9-12)

Part II: Grades 3-8

7th and 8th Grade

5th and 6th Grade

4th Grade

3rd Grade

ix

A special thank you to the judges of the 2009 Hill Country

Book Festival Writing Competition:

> Dr. Abbe Boring
> Dr. Roger Busfield
> Rev. Milton Jordan
> Connie Miller
> Helen Nardecchia
> Jane Thompson

Special thanks is also extended to Paula Brock, GISD

Secondary Language Arts Coordinator for her assistance

with the writing competition, grades 9-12.

@Georgetown, Texas

X

Part I

Writing Competition

Youth Division

Grades 9 - 12

Writing Prompt

Perhaps because words have the power to thrill and challenge us, they also sustain us through some of life's most difficult trials—no more so for adults than for teenagers, who face their own unique circumstances in the maturation process. Who among you hasn't lashed out in anger at a friend who has betrayed a confidence or delighted in publicly humiliating you? Who hasn't smarted from a sibling's jealous, blistering accusation? Who hasn't lost a race with a sibling to borrow Dad's car keys just when you had planned to take your friends for pizza? Who hasn't watched a fellow student receive a school honor that you knew you had rightfully earned? Who hasn't choked back tears when your request for admission to the college of your dreams was denied in an impersonal form letter? Who hasn't felt hot tears flow across your heart when one of your parents forgets or breaks a promise to attend your dance recital or season play-off game? Who hasn't experienced the pain of grief at the loss of a friend or loved one in a car accident or other tragedy?

Through it all, what one word or phrase have you muttered silently, repeatedly to sustain you—keep you from falling apart, calm your nerves, strengthen your faith, give you hope, affirm your being? It could be a grandparent's adage, a club or team motto, a scripture, a song title or lyric. Through what source—be it a person, situation, conversation or personal thought—did you discover the magic word or phrase that brought you the solace you have needed in life? When and where did it first occur to you? How did it help you? In what other critical situations have you called upon that word or phrase for comfort? Does it still work for you?

High School students had up to two-and-one half hours to write their papers in a controlled environment.

**First Place Winner
Brett Fox**

Junior, Georgetown High School

SYNOPSIS OF THE PROMPT EACH CONTESTANT WAS ASKED TO ADDRESS: Perhaps because words have the power to thrill and challenge us, they also sustain us through some of life's most difficult trials. What one word or phrase has sustained, calmed, strengthened, encouraged, or affirmed you during such a time?

In Pursuit of Excellence

In the midst of the cold December air biting at my cheeks, I could only sigh a deep sigh of anguish as I tasted the bitterest of defeats. I was dressed in warm clothes, yet the wind moved right through my body as emotionally I hit rock bottom. A little sick to my stomach, with my pride taken out at the knees, I began to cry. I do not like to cry. It makes me feel exposed and weak, but in this instance I felt that it was justified.

I had just walked out of what I thought would be the best moment of my life. I had been thinking about colleges and heard that these people were the ones to consult about enrollment. They had a reputation for being the best of the best as a college placement agency. They talked with students and parents about grades, community service, and a few trivial expectations, and then essentially decided if students were likely to get into the college they wanted. I had set high expectations for myself. I am an AP student who works very hard and can manage to get good grades despite not being naturally smart. I had my eye on Yale University and never let my vision falter. My parents were supportive yet a little hesitant because they did not want me to set "unachievable" goals for myself.

When we went into this firm, all was right with the world. I had my dream and nothing was going to wake me up to reality, or so I thought. After our little meeting with a smug, middle-aged woman, she stared at my transcript for the longest moment of my life, looked up and flatly said no. Not only no, but that I had absolutely zero chance of getting into this prestigious school. My parents sighed sadly for me but almost expected this and took the news quite calmly.

I was shattered. I had a hard time breathing and my stomach seemed to be in my throat. We walked out calmly and got down the street when I started to cry. My tears seemed to sting more than anything that woman could have said to me. I was disappointed in myself for crying because it was as if I accepted her judgment of my abilities. My parents remained solemnly quiet, and we slipped into our car and had a very melancholy drive home. My dad tried to be encouraging and had me watch *Rudy,* but it did no good.

The house was dead quiet for a few days as we completely digested the discouraging news. My mind was racing, and I found this most true when I lay down to go to sleep. I turned over and over every part of that day. *Was she right? Am I stupid? Why does it seem that no one supports me?* I had yet to find any peace. The days dragged by when I stumbled across an NBA commercial with a quote from Gandhi. At first I smirked and thought it would be another of his famous quotes people had devalued.

When the italicized script came on the screen, however, it hit me like a rock and really created ripples inside my soul. It read, "What lies ahead of you and what lies behind you is nothing compared to what lies within you." I had never heard that quote before, but now I use it almost as my personal motto. It gave me hope, but it also gave me a slap across the face to the reality of my situation. If I wanted to go to Yale, it was going to be because of **me**. Not the woman at the agency, not my friends or my parents, but me! If I moped all day because of someone else's judgment, maybe I didn't deserve to go to Yale, but if I worked hard and really became something on my own accord, I would be accepted to that university.

That quote really helped me through that time, and I became obsessed with that message. It was the first stepping-stone to where I am now. I began to read Ralph Waldo Emerson, who is my hero, and his essays on self-reliance only reinforced my thoughts. These two people really made me think. *What does it mean to be somebody? Can you think for yourself and become what you want because of your will and purpose? Will you step up to the*

challenge and make the best of circumstances even when rotten people try to tear you down? I churned through all these ideas in my mind and came out a much more positive person. They did not give me a free pass though. Believing in the power of dreams isn't going to get me into Yale, but determination, hard work and an unbreakable spirit will.

Every day since I came across Gandhi's words, I think back at how much I have changed, starting with that one commercial. Whenever I feel down or beat, I can look at this quote as a nice way of saying "suck it up" and as my way of knowing that I'm not failing, just falling. The important part is that I got knocked down five times but got up six. "What lies behind me and what lies ahead of me is nothing compared to what lies within me."

Second Place Winner
Kate Barnekow

Junior, Georgetown High School

SYNOPSIS OF THE PROMPT EACH CONTESTANT WAS ASKED TO ADDRESS: Perhaps because words have the power to thrill and challenge us, they also sustain us through some of life's most difficult trials. What one word or phrase has sustained, calmed, strengthened, encouraged, or affirmed you during such a time?

Before

Everything that you, he, she, they, we, I have experienced has been experienced by someone else, somewhere else, at some time before. No matter what you may be going through or dealing with, someone else at some other time has encountered the same. To some, this could seem a statement of exaggeration or a common cliché. To others, it may invoke a feeling of helplessness, of being too small for the world around them, of insignificance. To me, it's a reminder that I'm going to be okay, something I often seem to forget or merely fail to see. It's all been done before.

I can't say I've ever received an epiphany or anything of the sort. Thoughts, emotions, and realizations have never come to me suddenly. They seem to work themselves out in my brain over a period of time: weeks, months, maybe years. That said, I don't remember the first time I heard these five words. I don't remember the first time I truly registered the worth of these five words, and I don't remember the first time that these five words helped me. This isn't that I was careless with my memories. It's that these instances weren't significant enough in the long run to impress me. What the words needed was time, time to prove to me their relevance and eventual unfaltering support. There must have been years between each of these three events. At this time, the memories of these explicit occasions have been lost. What remains is the important part. What remains is their effect.

I remember a time when I was nervous. I was told to take a deep breath, hold it a few seconds, and then let go. I didn't think it would help, but I complied. I did so merely because I wanted to prove that it wouldn't help. But what happened when I let that giant gulp of air out was a flood of immense relief and almost staggering calm. It was as if I'd been holding on to such massive weight for so long that it was on the cusp of slipping painfully out of my hands. Someone unnamed had suddenly lifted that something, effortlessly. As it happens, I was in the fourth grade and was nervous about my first "real" basketball game, but that's irrelevant. The pertinent element is that that sensation stuck with me through all of these years, and it's the one self-induced feeling that I could rightfully compare to the one brought on by these words:

It's all been done before.

I could fill a book with personal, mostly dull and tedious anecdotes concerning times that I've called upon this phrase. The problem is that you wouldn't want to read it, and I wouldn't want to write it. It's not the small things now and in the past that matter. They alone would prove nothing. The proof lies where no one can catch a glimpse of it or feel it. The proof is that I know within that I can keep myself moving forward, thinking, and living.

I may not speak them aloud or even consciously think the individual words, but anytime I feel myself begin to waver or lose sight of who I am or where I want to go, the reminder comes to me that I'm not doing anything that I or anyone else can't do. Then somehow, I'm able to get back to where I need and want to be.

It's all been done before.

It's all been done before!

Third Place Winner

Alicia Capps

Sophomore, Home Schooled

SYNOPSIS OF THE PROMPT EACH CONTESTANT WAS ASKED TO ADDRESS: Perhaps because words have the power to thrill and challenge us, they also sustain us through some of life's most difficult trials. What one word or phrase has sustained, calmed, strengthened, encouraged, or affirmed you during such a time?

Anything for You, Mary Jones

Heartbreak. It's a part of life; wherever you find love, you will find heartbreak. I certainly have had my fair share of it. It began with my love for the girl of my dreams, Mary Jones. I believed she was as taken with me as I had been with her. I, Ian Ron Johnson, was the man of her dreams - a firefighter, the one who would be daring enough to dash into any situation, no matter how hopeless it seemed, to rescue an endangered life. I was her hero; I was her soul mate. All this she had told me herself. And she was my passion. I would do anything for her, anything she asked; she could do no wrong in my eyes.

"Ian," she had said enthusiastically to me one day. "I want to see the inside of the fire station; I've always wanted to go into one."

"Anything for you, Mary Jones," I had replied, as always to her pleas. It was my way of saying "I love you, Mary Jones," and I meant it every time I said it. It was far more intense than I could ever express with any other words, my love for her.

As was her wish, I took her to see the inside of the fire station and to meet the guys, the true reason she had wanted to go. That was shortly before I found her with

Michael Oshay, when I was on my way back through the halls to my office. Her back being turned to me, I hadn't realized who she was when I first saw them. Michael had been seen with another blond before. However, I recognized the golden shoulder-length traces of curls and the elegant, slim figure; everything about her had been unmistakably familiar.

"Mary?" My tone had been unbelieving; I couldn't grasp the fact that my Mary, the love of my life, could be with any other man.

"Ian!" she had gasped, turning to face me, her rosy cheeks beginning to pale like faded pink chalk. The two deep blue pools of sapphire eyes were wide with shock and maybe a hint of fear. Her dainty hand was covering her pale lips.

"Ian, Buddy," Michael had said as carefree as ever.

"What's going on here?" was all I had managed to say. But I could see perfectly well what was going on here and I didn't want to believe my eyes. "You didn't love me?"

"I.... sound like a criminal." With that, she had turned and ran, leaving me trying to grasp what I had seen, and when I turned to confront Michael, he was already gone.

About a week passed, in which time I didn't hear from Mary Jones at all. Michael avoided me as much as possible, and for good reason. Though I hadn't liked him much before, my once medium-high tolerance for him had nearly completely vanished. Then the call came. The red emergency lights flashed, blinking like discolored lightning, and the sirens screamed as we got an urgent call to a fire on South Wind Street 57340, the exact same apartment complex where Mary Jones lived.

As was standard regulations, the boys and I geared up and headed out, zooming down Main Street to get to South Wind. Within fifteen minutes we arrived at the apartment complex. Jumping from the truck, the boys went to work pulling out the rope and hooking up to the fire hydrant.

A never-ending stream of smoke billowed out the windows, and flickering flames leaped from beneath them, striking at the sky outside. Already a shadow of charcoal darkened the areas around the windows, coating the white stone in filth. It looked like most of the inside of the building was already eaten away by the flames and beyond stopping; we were too late to save the building from its doom. Just as I was considering who was possibly still alive in there, I saw, in the window at the top floor, the silhouette of an elegant form lost in the smoke, saw it pounding against the closed window, saw it floundering back into the smoke, saw it collapsing. That was Mary's floor, the exact window above Mary's couch, her exact shape.

"Jake!" I called, my oxygen mask in my hands. He was at my side within seconds. "Mary's in there; I'm going in." He was my rescuing partner.

"I'm not going in there!" he cried. "Are you crazy?! That place is fixing to come down."

"But Mary's in there." There was no changing his mind. "Set up the ladder!" I commanded, and the boys set to work doing so.

Donning my oxygen mask, I lifted the sledgehammer and began climbing the towering wall as fast as I could to her window. I drew the sledgehammer back, swinging it at the window as hard as I could.

The glass shattered. The sledgehammer slipped out of my grasp and fell all the way down the length of ladder, but I had little time to think about that. I climbed through the window, the sound of my breathing loud in my ears due to the mask. The smoke was thick, and it was hard to see even a few inches in front of me. I plodded forward slowly, searching, when I found Mary's body on the floor.

Lifting her gently in my arms, I made my way back to the window and attempted to get her out when there was a loud "CRACK." It was like thunder, and I knew it meant that the place was coming down. The ceiling began to cave in behind me, slowly coming towards the window.

Throwing Mary and myself out the window, I shielded Mary with my body, allowing me to hit the ground first. The window collapsed moments behind me, and the building began to tumble down, flames leaping higher than ever, smoke pouring into the sky. The fall seemed to take an eternity until at last my body hit the ground with a thud. Pain shot through me, and the wind was knocked out of me as my world blackened.

I woke in a white room, my body feeling like lead, stiff from the casts stuck on my left arm and leg. I noticed a figure to my right, one dark thing in that room of white. Looking over I saw her, Mary, nose and cheeks red with crying, sapphire blue eyes watery. Silence reigned until at last her wavering voice broke it.

"I'm sorry, Ian," she sniffed as the tears welled in her eyes. "After what I did,… you saved me."

"Anything for you, Mary Jones." And I really meant it, each word of it, with every fiber of my being, with every bit of passion in me. Heartbreak is the inevitable part of

life; you can't avoid it. But it doesn't last forever.

Fourth Place

Madison Kruger

Freshman
Georgetown Ninth Grade Center

SYNOPSIS OF THE PROMPT EACH CONTESTANT WAS ASKED TO ADDRESS: Perhaps because words have the power to thrill and challenge us, they also sustain us through some of life's most difficult trials. What one word or phrase has sustained, calmed, strengthened, encouraged, or affirmed you during such a time?

Just Smile

Have you ever had one of those ghastly days when nothing seems to go your way? Maybe you wake up late, skip breakfast, run out of time to swing by Starbucks, and are still late to work. We all have those days and we are all faced with difficult times. You might find yourself wondering how people are happy if they are faced with particularly challenging situations. The answer is not luck or wealth or destiny; the true reason that people are happy is the way they respond to a tricky challenge. For some of us, the ability to do well in a tough situation comes easy, but for most of us, lifting our spirits in a bad situation is complicated. Until a clever friend offered me some wise words of advice, I was one of those people who couldn't find a way to lift my spirits when life seemed to head the wrong direction.

I was nine when I moved to a new school for the first time. Coming from a small town where I had known every other person in my school, I was overwhelmed with the thought of starting out alone. On my first day of third grade, I went to school with fresh new clothes, a new lunch box, and shiny new shoes; but on this first day at a new school, I didn't wear the same shiny smile that I had always worn on the first day of school in years past. I wore the look of an extremely nervous third grader. For the first time in my young life, I was faced with a strange environment. As I walked into my new school, my heart didn't swell with joy; instead, my eyes swelled with hot tears.

My first days of third grade, I am sorry to say, went terribly; I was unable to function without my caring friends. I went through five lunches and five horrific recesses on my own; all the while, I bawled like a lost baby calf.

One Saturday night about a week after the first day of school, my best friend Jill gave me some of the best advice I think any nine-year-old could ever have offered. As I sat talking on the phone to Jill in my cozy bedroom, hot salty tears began to fall down my small cheeks while I told her about the rotten first week I had endured. I told her about all of the lonely lunches and giggleless recesses of the past week. While I talked, I could almost hear Jill's heart listening to me blubber on and on.

When I had finished telling about those tough days, the phone line grew quiet while Jill's juvenile mind took in all of my despair. After a few moments, Jill finally spoke up, and with her petite voice, she asked me a question that I hadn't seen coming. "You have been at school for five days now, you have sat at lunch and at recess alone five times, and you have shed an unimaginable number of tears; but I must ask how many times have you smiled?"

To this day, I can still remember the shock I got after hearing those few little words. For the second time that evening, the phone line grew silent as I thought in disbelief about my week. Through the five rough days, I had not thought once about smiling; all I had thought about

30

was how much I missed my old friends. The more I thought about it, the more I knew that my answer was weak. I had not smiled once in all of the hours I had spent in that school building. Timidly, I squeaked out my answer, "I have not smiled once."

For the next few minutes, my friend taught me a skill that would come in handy the rest of my life. Jill explained to me the power of a smile and the magic of such a simple expression. Jill told me that a smile is magical. When you smile, you show others many things; you show that you are a kind, happy and, most of all, friendly person. Jill asked me to smile at just one person and to share the results with her. "Just smile and magical things can happen," Jill exclaimed before we hung up our phones.

The following Monday, I listened to Jill's advice. Instead of crying and sitting alone, I smiled at the girl in the seat next to me. She, just as Jill had predicted, smiled back. At lunch, I sat next to the girl. She introduced herself as Molly, and from the moment she told me her name, we talked and talked and talked.

That night I called Jill to tell her about my amazing day. I thanked her for being such a wonderful friend and praised her for her great knowledge.

I have never eaten lunch alone since that first week of third grade. Molly and I are still inseparable friends to this day. Some people would say that I just got lucky, that it was destiny for me to meet my best friend in third grade. I, on the other hand, don't believe so. I believe that those two words *just smile* are what brought up my spirits and encouraged me to start a friendship. I had high spirits in a negative situation but listened to my friend's encouraging words. Now I live by the phrase "just smile" every day because I believe that with high hopes and a happy facial

expression, anyone can be a happy person.

Awards of Merit
(in alphabetical order)

Louis Capps

Sophomore, Home Schooled

SYNOPSIS OF THE PROMPT EACH CONTESTANT WAS ASKED TO ADDRESS: Perhaps because words have the power to thrill and challenge us, they also sustain us through some of life's most difficult trials. What one word or phrase has sustained, calmed, strengthened, encouraged, or affirmed you during such a time?

The Unchangeable Phrase

"The Lord is my shepherd, whom shall I fear."

These unchangeable words come from the Bible. I have

said them over and over to sustain myself in hard times.

They are a foundation upon which I am able to keep my sanity.

Finding the perfect phrase is not an easy task. Many words, thoughts, and expressions have tried to stop me from finding mine. At first, when I was younger, all I would need to say was the word *Jesus.* That word brought comfort and warmth to my soul. Although this name worked well, my maturing mind needed something more, something longer. With this need constantly haunting me, I decided to change the name to a phrase. It became "Jesus, help me." After much thought, I was satisfied that this would always be enough, but alas, it wasn't.

One night, I was carrying a bag of garbage to the end of our extremely long driveway, where I would then throw it into our trash can. As I started down the drive, I heard dogs barking somewhere in the neighborhood, the whistle of the wind in the trees, and the creaking sound of our neighbors' miniature windmill. The night seemed friendly, but as I walked out of the reach of light shining from my house, the night took a drastic turn for the worse. There was no moon to guide me, and my thoughts and mind began to play tricks on me. There were new sounds, completely different and tremendously scary. There were the sound of werewolves howling just around the corner and waiting to take me captive; the sound of creatures whistling to each other and singing songs of victory over their next human meal; and even the sound of evil knights, adorned with armor as black as night and with their dark blades drawn, approaching me so that they could kill me, take my body once I was dead and claim it as their next and greatest trophy.

Within the turmoil of my mind, I managed to seize a few words, "Jesus, help me." As I said these three words over and over, the storm in my mind began to calm. As it calmed, however, I realized that I had not been saying, "Jesus, help me." Instead, I had been saying, "The Lord is my Shepherd, whom shall I fear." These words brought even more comfort and warmth to my soul. This was an unchangeable phrase. No longer would evil knights with their black armor and dark swords haunt me, no longer would creatures with whistling voices crave my flesh, no longer would werewolves desire me as their next meal, and no longer would my mind play tricks on me. I was now free.

This was my journey to find an unchangeable phrase. Now that I have found it, I use it in my life almost every day.

Corie Cercla

Junior, Georgetown High School

SYNOPSIS OF THE PROMPT EACH CONTESTANT WAS ASKED TO ADDRESS: Perhaps because words have the power to thrill and challenge us, they also sustain us through some of life's most difficult trials. What one word or phrase has sustained, calmed, strengthened, encouraged, or affirmed you during such a time?

"Don't Worry About a Thing!"

Allowing myself to envisage the thought of possessing what others called a friend, my melancholy eyes drifted from each smiling face to the next. These faces grinned as if they were mocking me while my envious gaze descended upon them, those loathsome wretches. A malevolent, chaotic twist of emotions, twinged with malice, whirled about my mind — twirled, swirled, and bubbled over into a pot where a witch roosted as she stirred her foaming, spurting brew. My needy heart was capitulating to the voracious demons of grief, unfathomable loneliness, and self-repugnance and was falling into a hole the devil himself carved out of worm-infested grounds. Could anything upon this utopian Earth bestow a reason for my existence?

My listless self attempted a response that gave one of the Seven Deadly Sins (Envy) its absolute dominance over me: to smile. A smile signified happiness that was falsely molded into my face day in and out. What was the "happiness" that my decaying heart desired? I called it into question, this foreign emotion that gave these smiling wretches their source of strength. I knew not what it meant to be valued by the shadows that rushed past my seemingly non-existent self.

The smile I was to attempt made me race straight into what would be a catastrophic train wreck. How could I pretend a smile to the wretches about me? Being a conformist to them made my blood boil in my veins, my brows angle as my sheltered anger rose and my lips repressed screams of my gnawing emotions.

"Watch out!" a girl's frantic voice shouted behind me once or twice. Taking no heed to the warning, I did nothing until what felt as if a train slammed into me. I fell forward and landed on the school's cold tile floor. Beneath me was the icy chill of winter and on top of me was someone apologizing time and time again before she could even get up.

Sitting up, I looked at her strangely. My curiosity suppressed my anger as I watched the girl carefully and wondered what would happen next. Would the girl just get up and leave?

"I'm so sorry," she began again as she grinned with childish embarrassment. "I was running because I thought I was being chased by something, and I didn't pay attention to where I was going." She paused as she scanned my body for any injuries as if just remembering that I was the one pinned between the floor and her. "I'm glad you're okay."

Jolted by an unfamiliar feeling, I felt my lips perk up at the corners, as my eyes softened. A small giggle escaped from my grinning lips as the girl flushed tomato red again. "I'm all right," I replied, as the rims of my eyes began to glaze over with unfamiliar tears.

"Oh no!" she clamored with hysterics as her hands frantically flailed up and down. "Are you in pain? Do you need a Band Aid? How about a . . ."

Cutting her off, I giggled and broke into an all out laugh of simple yet complete bliss. "Don't worry about... "

Finishing my sentence, she sang, "...about a thing because every little thing is gonna to be alright!"

The girl's look shot me an invitation to continue as my laugher peeked. The Bob Marley song plastered a smile on my face as the two of us sang together down the once long, forsaken hallways.

I thought as the girl next to me again flashed her tender grin that maybe smiling wasn't so bad, that being with a friend made a smile worthwhile.

Since that day, when we clashed like two linemen on a football team, the girl and I have become best friends.

I still sing "Don't Worry about a Thing." Although it may conjure memories of once being a feeble outcast, the song gives me strength when I need it most. It is her and my reminder that no matter how abominable the situation may be, "every little thing is gonna be alright."

Erinn Fitzgerald

Freshman, Georgetown Ninth Grade Center

SYNOPSIS OF THE PROMPT EACH CONTESTANT WAS ASKED TO ADDRESS: Perhaps because words have the power to thrill and challenge us, they also sustain us through some of life's most difficult trials. What one word or phrase has sustained, calmed, strengthened, encouraged, or affirmed you during such a time?

All Because I Said "I Can Do It"

The words *I can do it* seem to be a commonplace phrase. For many, the words have lost their luster, the shine they put into the human mind, and the inspiration that empowers youngsters to dare actions that those older than youth deem silly and intolerable in public.

But to children and teenagers, *I can do it* are the words of heroes, the underdog pulling through and making it to the top. They are the words of dreams come to life. After all, "We are the music makers, and we are the dreamers of dreams" (Willy Wonka from *Charlie and the Chocolate Factory*).

As a child, I was, to say the least, energetic. I would not go to sleep. I would not calm down. I demanded praise for my every action and attempted to grab the attention of everyone I could. I charged through life like a whirlwind, straight into the "wall" and through to the other side of any fear, any problem. I was a classic example of a frisky troublemaker, from infancy to double digits.

At one point in elementary school, we went as a school to San Gabriel Park for the day. A girl whom I tagged along with accompanied me to the largest climbable tree we could find. The youngest kid we knew who could make it to the top was a third grader at another school.

"Don't even try to climb that one. You're too small."

I whirled around to see a second-grade boy standing behind us. My face contorted into a stubborn frown. Just to prove to this boy, whom I didn't even know, that he was wrong, I pushed up the short sleeves of my shirt like characters did in my favorite cartoon, *Jackie Chan Adventures*; and I walked up to the base of the tree to start my ascent.

I was already well on my way through my climb before I could hear the debate about if and when I'd resign and return to the ground.

"She won't make it to the top of that tree, will she?" my classmate on the ground asked as my scrubby kindergartener body shimmied up the tree.

"There's no way! She's too small to reach!" the second grader replied when my small arms failed to reach a large branch above me. Naturally being a troublemaker, I was hot-tempered and never liked to be told I couldn't do something.

"I can do it!" I shouted down. Standing upright on a wide limb and grasping the thick and rigid bark with one hand, I made a jump for it. As my little arms wrapped around the branch and I clambered onto the sprig, the juveniles below me gasped and murmured doubts like "I didn't think she'd do it!" and "I thought she'd give up!"

Their words put a smirk on my determined, neophyte face, the feat I'd overcome to get there giving me an adrenaline rush. Getting excited over the praise I'd won from my performance, I pushed upward. Soon my head extended through the canopy of leaves and gave me a view of seemingly endless sky, the sunlight bright and gold, the playgrounds and swing sets scattered around the field.

"What's it look like up there?" asked the second grader.

I poked my head back down through the leaves and retorted haughtily, "If you want to know so bad, come up here and see it!"

He got sore from what I'd said and stormed away from my classmate standing below. She cried, "Come back down before the teacher sees you!"

I began my descent carelessly, making close calls on my way down. I blundered, lost my grip and footing, got scraped up, and even fell at one point, a large branch rescuing me from a far-off and painful drop with the full force of gravity. Every time I slipped or got grazed, my consort beneath the boughs of the tree yelled, "Do you need me to get help?"

And every time, my bellicose blood compelled me, up until I made it back to the ground, to shout back, "I can do it!"

The words of human beings hold more power than most of us comprehend. Sometimes, if we keep at it, saying words over and over again with all our hearts can make us daring enough to make the words come true.

The words *I can do it* have more meaning to me than any others do, for they can release my captive dreams, make them blend with reality, and help me to realize the wishes deepest in my heart. All who truly believe the same shall be granted their wishes as well, and their minds will

find joy and peace, the true essence of life.

Alana Hilliard

Senior, Georgetown High School

SYNOPSIS OF THE PROMPT EACH CONTESTANT WAS ASKED TO ADDRESS: Perhaps because words have the power to thrill and challenge us, they also sustain us through some of life's most difficult trials. What one word or phrase has sustained, calmed, strengthened, encouraged, or affirmed you during such a time?

Just Keep Swimming

The light blue skies were spotted with white cotton balls. The sun's rays reached down and danced warmly on my skin. A cool breeze swirled playfully at my feet as I walked home from my best friend's house. The song we'd been obsessed with for months still played on repeat in my mind, as though an iPod were lodged in my brain keeping the song on repeat nonstop. *"I can't believe the drama that*

I'm in. The flood is getting stronger, but they don't know that I know how to swim." Escape the Fate's lyrics to "The Flood," flowed effortlessly through my mind, and I began to sing them as I walked.

I turned the corner to my street. I felt so good that I decided to run toward my home. I flung the door open and flew inside. Everything seemed normal at first, yet it felt as though "the flood" really was about to come. The house was completely empty and dark. Usually the television was on as my older brother watched it from the couch or my mother was cooking dinner. I called to find an answer to no avail.

I found my sister on her bed staring blankly at the wall as I entered her room. "What's wrong?" I asked, plopping down next to her.

"You didn't hear?" Her eyes were huge. Her face gave her the appearance of a ghost.

"Hear what?"

"Mom and Dad didn't tell you?"

"Tell me what?"

"Blake was in an accident." She whispered.

I let out a laugh. "Yeah, right."

"I'm serious!"

"Whoa, calm yourself down. Is he okay?"

"I don't know. Mom was crying and Dad's face was stone. They said they were going to the hospital."

"The hospital?" My heart sank down to my stomach before making the trip up to my throat where it pounded mercilessly. Hospitals were for sick and hurt people. My brother was in the hospital! I freaked out. I refused to believe it.

"He hurt someone too." Her voice was hollow. I shivered despite how warm it was in the house. The ice that had just engulfed my body was obviously not aware of this fact.

"Who?"

"Someone from your school. I don't know who."

I closed my eyes and willed myself that everything would be okay. *I can't believe the drama that I'm in. The flood is getting stronger.* It was real now. My brother and someone else were hurt…badly enough to go to the hospital. Tears filled my eyes. I willed them to stay back. I didn't want to cry in front of Camille. They didn't want to listen. They wanted to be free and run like two rivers down my face.

They don't know that I know how to swim. That's all I could think about now. "I know how to swim…" I whispered. Camille stared at me. Suddenly, her face finally had some life added back to it.

"What does swimming have to do with any of this?" She half yelled. "Blake is hurt and all you can think about is swimming? You're so twisted."

I laughed. The tears were gone. I knew that despite what had happened I had to be strong for Cami. She was my inspiration. The tears disappeared from my eyes.

"Want to go watch TV with me? Maybe your favorite show is on."

"You hate Disney!"

I smiled. At ten, she was still a slave to the network. "I want to watch it with you now." I stood up, offering her my hand. "Do you want to see what's on?" She nodded and took my hand. I led her down the stairs and to the living room, where we spent the next three hours lost in imagination to the shows of innocence.

Our parents got home with Blake. He had some broken ribs and a collapsed lung but was otherwise okay. The other kid was okay too with some cuts and bruises. I had been so focused keeping my sister occupied that I'd lost all consciousness about my brother. I laughed to myself. Turns out that I did know how to swim after all and I'd proven that.

That very line always plays in my mind when I feel as if I'm lost. When I feel there is no way out and I'm just going to drown in the flood of events, I remember that I know how to swim. I've used these lyrics more times than I can count. They always pop into my head when I need them most. When there are a lot of problems going on at school with my friends. When I'm feeling like giving up on a subject that's too difficult for me understand. The day my best friend almost died. Every time someone tries to keep me down. *They don't know that I know how to swim.* These words inspire me. In the words of a very wise fish, "Just keep swimming." It might just save you from the flood.

Nina Klaser

Junior, Georgetown High School

SYNOPSIS OF THE PROMPT EACH CONTESTANT WAS ASKED TO ADDRESS: Perhaps because words have the power to thrill and challenge us, they also sustain us through some of life's most difficult trials. What one word or phrase has sustained, calmed, strengthened, encouraged, or affirmed you during such a time?

Lift Me Up Again

He screamed at her from the hall. Called her everything lower than trash, and she sat there like stone. He yelled and told her everything she'd never be. After seventeen years of hearing it, she no longer had the need to shed tears. She had let enough flow to dry herself out completely. He said she was nothing and always would be nothing.

This was a typical morning for Haley Williams. She usually woke up at seven o'clock, threw on the first pieces of clothing her hand touched, eluded her stepfather, Steven, and walked to school. Today, she wasn't so inconspicuous. Drunk again, Steven stayed up all night waiting for the pleasure of demeaning Haley to a frog carcass covered in preservative and awaiting dissection by a day-dreaming, I-don't-know-what-I'm-doing, thirteen-year-old boy. Steven somehow loved seeing Haley shut down and becoming this degraded carcass, and she knew it too. The day she learned it was the day the tears stopped flowing.

This time, assuming that her stepfather was done with his aimless rant, Haley made her way to school. He was still screaming when she noiselessly shut the door. Her walk to school wasn't long or short, but just enough to let Haley get a grip on life again. The walk was her intermission from the world, no one to yell at her, no one to bug her with the day's gossip, no one trying to get her on that date. It was all just her.

"Haley!" a voice called to her from afar. Soon the silhouette of a boy began to appear.

"Hey, Peter," Haley called back when he was closer. "What are you doing over here?" Haley asked, noting that she was only about five minutes from her house and ten minutes from the school.

"I just thought I'd come keep you company. How's my favorite girl?" Peter smiled his big goofy, toothy smile as he threw his arm around Haley's shoulders.

Smiling as well as she could, Haley replied, "I've been better, Pete; Steven got drunk again…" Her attempt at a smile deteriorated and she looked to the sidewalk.

"Oh, do you wanna talk about it?" Pete asked. He knew what happened when Steven lost himself in his bottle. Pete only wished he could make up for her bad start to the day.

"No, I'd rather not think about it…. Anyway, did you do the chemistry homework?" Desperately, Haley tried to change the subject.

"Nope, never have, never will!" Pete exclaimed with misplaced joy. "As a matter of fact, you and me are going to spend a day off." Pete smiled that goofy grin.

"What are you planning?" Haley asked through a timid smile.

Pete stood in front of her, his hands on her shoulders. He looked her in the eye and said, "You and me are going to skip school and have some fun today. We will go to the arcade, grab some pizza, catch a movie, and make up for your crappy morning. Okay?" Pete's tone told her that she wasn't telling him no.

"Pete, you don't have to do that," she said, looking down at the concrete.

"But I want to, and besides this'll be fun!" Pete pleaded with her.

"Fine," Haley answered.

Pete celebrated and grabbed her hand, and they ran together, laughing, in the opposite direction of the school.

They did exactly what Pete had planned. They laughed the whole time and gorged themselves on greasy pizza. They battled and vanquished the unrelenting ghosts of Pac Man, and they watched a movie about a robot finding the love he had always dreamed of. They didn't want the day to end. Feeling a mutual sadness, they hesitantly parted ways.

Haley had made a decision that morning, one that would hopefully make Steven feel like the frog he made her into. But after the day with Pete, now she wasn't so sure. She had forgotten how much she adored having her friend by her side. Today was going to be Haley's perfect day to die, but Pete had made it her perfect day to live.

Sighing with content, Haley changed into her pajamas and drifted to sleep with a smile across her face.

Pete smiled too; he just hoped that tomorrow she would be there. He knew what Haley had been planning to do. He just hoped that the day they had spent together would change her mind. After all, what is a friend for if not to lift you up again when you crash to the ground and can't get back up? Pete was elated that he was able to lift her up again, and he'd do it time after time for however long it took.

Sean McDonald

Freshman, Georgetown Ninth Grade Center

SYNOPSIS OF THE PROMPT EACH CONTESTANT WAS ASKED TO ADDRESS: Perhaps because words have the power to thrill and challenge us, they also sustain us through some of life's most difficult trials. What one word or phrase has sustained, calmed, strengthened, encouraged, or affirmed you during such a time?

The Power of Words

There is a certain power in words, whether they reside in a prayer or an heroic chant that pours out its sweetness from a teammate's lips. They can be a small, soft phrase or a booming line that buoys thousands for a cause. Martin Luther King, Jr. knew this. His "I Have a Dream" speech inspired millions and inspires still. As for me, a simple and common saying brings into my chest a fire that longs to burst forth and prove itself. This saying is "never give up."

As most young people are until their teen years, I was a simple boy with simple goals. I was naive, impatient, and easily discouraged when the blunt edge of an obstacle planted itself in my face. As time passed, however, the words I had heard so many times continued to poke and prod what little determination I had then. The initial sensation was that of conflict. Do I relax and ignore my situation or give it another go and see what I can do with just a bit of perseverance.

One major example of this conflict was my short time in kindergarten. A normally quiet and shy young man at home, I was a boisterous and passionate ruffian at school. I had to experiment with everything I came across, from dissecting a hornet's nest to lighting some papers on fire with a suspicious and transparently disguised lighter. Curiosity was my strength, but it was frowned upon at Lakewood Elementary, as similar "incidents" had apparently occurred due to other curious students. My skill in all subjects and my voracity as a reader, with the reading capacity of a high school student, "drove me home" academically; but in a teacher's vigilant eye, I was behind other students in my behavior towards the rights of minors and so-called "authority." I was a bug splattered on her clean windshield of students. But those inspiring words persisted with increasing authority. Being irritated at the "boss lady's" demands, I vowed to become the perfect student.

With higher grades came more homework. "Never give up" became a shout pulsing in time with my heartbeat.

I studiously worked at my schoolwork, my sports, my personal life, and my relationship with my teachers.

I advanced through the grades, from elementary to middle school, from middle school to junior high school, and above. An unsatisfactory grade on an assignment or a missed shot in sports never shook me. I set lofty goals, and my eyes fixed upon them with fiery intensity. Now I am a freshman in high school, working to graduate as valedictorian and continue to college to receive both bachelor and post-graduate degrees.

Just because some goals seem to reach beyond the swirling clouds does not mean they are unobtainable or even unrealistic. I just remember that those wonderful words have crossed the mouths of almost every ancient and modern hero: *never give up*. I truly believe in the message behind those words.

If that three-word saying has gotten humanity where

it is now, why can't it work for you?

Never Give Up!

Annie McTigue

Freshman, Georgetown Ninth Grade Center

SYNOPSIS OF THE PROMPT EACH CONTESTANT WAS ASKED
TO ADDRESS: Perhaps because words have the power to thrill and
challenge us, they also sustain us through some of life's most difficult
trials. What one word or phrase has sustained, calmed, strengthened,
encouraged, or affirmed you during such a time?

The Power of Breathing

In through the nose, out through the mouth.
Something about the coolness of my breath as I exhale
always seems to calm me. The sensations of tightness, of
stress, of negative feelings remind me to do one thing:
breathe. It soothes the soul, cools the mind, and brings
within it comfort in difficult situations.

All around me were sobs, bloodshot eyes, and muffled cries. It was all I could do to contain myself. I didn't start to "lose it" until the picture slideshows appeared on the VCR. I felt that a river of emotions had broken the floodgates in my heart, and all at once a rage of uncontrollable feelings started to pour out. I shut my eyes and desperately looked inside my heart for something, anything, to keep me sane. It was then, at my mother's funeral, that I had discovered the word *breathe*.

As soon as I began to concentrate on breathing, it seemed as though everything was serene, and I knew I was going to be okay. When times become hard and we think we might lose control, we often times forget to breathe.

When we are uncomfortable, we try to acclimate to the ease the situation. For instance, if it is too hot, we turn on the fan or lower the thermostat. The feeling of colder air usually cools us down to a more comfortable temperature. Why wouldn't we do the same—cool down—for the wellbeing of our emotions? The same concept applies to breathing. When we remind ourselves just to stop and breathe for a moment, we allow a break from everyday stresses and just think for a moment.

It was Halloween night, and some friends of mine and I decided to go running. I had run about fifteen yards before I felt something weird under my foot. Assuming it was nothing, I ignored it and continued running. By the time we had reached my best friend's house, my foot began to sting. When I looked down, I noticed a trail of blood leading to my foot. It looked as if a little kid had painted my foot with red Tempura paint and put fake bullet holes on my toe. By the time I realized what was happening, I began to feel dizzy. I closed my eyes and told myself to breathe. I was told I might need stitches and possibly corrective surgery, but I was okay and remained calm because I remembered to breathe.

To this day, I still continue to remind myself to breathe. I may not always do as well as I would like in something, but I never become too worked-up about anything because in the end I will always be all right. In the occasional instances when I do find myself on the edge, I realize that I just need to take a deep breath.

If you ever feel that you can't handle something or you're just in a bad place, mentally or physically, just remind yourself to breathe. When things become difficult, just stop and breathe and allow yourself some time to think of solutions to problems. There is nothing you can't do when you remember to breathe—"in through the nose, out through the mouth."

Part II

Writing Competition for Young Authors

Grades 3 - 8

Writing Prompt for Young Writers
(Grades 3-8)

Prompt: *It was magical!*

Example: Write about an experience that seemed magical for you or for a fictional character like winning a race or receiving an award or prize.

Write about a place that seemed magical like a library, a store, or an amusement park.

Write about a special thing that seemed magical to you.

Enjoy your story writing! We hope it is a magical experience for you, and we look forward to reading it!

Elementary students were allowed to work on their stories independently and submit them to the program coordinator upon completion.

First Place - 7th and 8th Grade Category

Carley May

8th Grade, Forbes Middle School

All my life I have wanted to become a veterinarian. My one goal has been to watch puppies being born before I go to high school. I have been to 49 of the 50 states and hit three of the seven continents, but I have saved my magical experience for the gift of life. From the first time I can remember, I have known if I ever get the chance to experience the birth of puppies, it would be my most magical experience.

It was Monday, March 2, 2009. I was in my piano lesson. My mom was on her computer calculating the exact day that Missy, my miniature dachshund, would have her puppies. When I was finished with my lesson, I ran upstairs to hear the news. My mom said, "Everyone, I have an announcement to make; Missy's puppies will be due March 5, 2009! Hey, Mackenzie, that is your birthday, too!" Mackenzie is my baby sister. I was excited because it was only three days until three bundles of joy would join our family.

I had a reading project due that Friday as well, so I had to read right that instant. I ran downstairs to get my book. I forgot that I had read my book the night before in my sister's room, so my book was really in there.

I walked into my room where both Missy and Oscar were. They were both in their crates that I had moved into my room for when Missy had her puppies. Then I smelled something really bad. That's when I remembered that I hadn't taken the dogs out for a while. I went to see if one of them had gone to the bathroom in the crate. I saw something green. It was disgusting, but then I saw it move. I panicked and then I screamed at the top of my lungs, "Mom, Missy had a puppy!"

My whole family came running down the stairs. My mom and I got in the crate with our shaky hands while my dad called the owner of the sire. My mom and I tried to get the birth sack off with our bare hands (believe it or not, those things are actually hard to break).

Then my dad reached the owners and said, "Um, um …. Missy's having puppies! Talk to mamma!"

The lady on the phone said, "Now try and stay calm. Did you try to get the sack off?"

"Yes! Yes! We did that – what now!" my mom said.

When the sire's owner was satisfied mom understood her directions, she said, "Okay, watch her and see what happens."

"Okay, bye."

Now it was up to us to keep the puppies alive.

Finally, we got the sack off, but the puppy was not breathing. My mom and I were hitting the puppy on the head, nose, and even its chest. Then Missy pulled the umbilical cord so that the puppy could take a breath, and it did. Apparently, when the umbilical cord is still attached the mother is breathing for the puppy.

That's when my dad said, "Okay, let nature take its course; everyone back up."

Everyone let out a big sigh of relief and watched Missy have two more beautiful puppies.

After a few days, Missy finally let us hold the puppies. The puppies were so fun to have around.

Well, it did turn out to be one of the most magical experiences for me, especially since I want to be a veterinarian. Missy turned out to be a great mother. All of the puppies are safe and in loving homes.

Award of Merit - 7th and 8th Grade Category

Krista Capps

8th Grade, Home Schooled

Peace in My Storm

(Fiction)

I basked in the glow of the sun, which was filtering through the circular stained glass window far above me. A chilly wind swept past my kneeling form, but it skulked away unnoticed. Silence held the stone ruins in a quiet spell. Weeping willows swished gently with the calming breeze. Rye grass squeezed its way through various cracks in the stone floor of the old chapel. The small church must have been made centuries ago, though some of the sturdy stone remained, slowly deteriorating with time.

It may have seemed a desolate, solitary place for many who passed, but for me, it was a serene sanctuary. It was a place to wonder of His enchanting grace, and magical mercy, but most of all, His never-ending being of love, His beauty shone everywhere.

The grass whispered His name as the wind sang of His virtues. The nearby steam burbled forth exaltations, as the birds cried out stories of the Jesus of Galilee. Yes, it was a magical place, and no one could tell me less.

The Lord's presence was there with me, and I could feel it. It was here that I found my deepest peace, my understanding in life, and my soul's one true desire. But it was not only a place of continual peace, for I had poured out laments from my heart during times of trouble.

It was also a place I could come with my sorrows over my mother's death. I remember it well. On the way through the misty forest on the out-skirts of my secret place, I would hear her whisper. She would call to me, from an evil place, where I knew she could only be. Many times, I had tried to save her, and many times, I told of His love. I told her of heaven's love, and the hatred in hell. I cried, I prayed, and I begged her to see the light. However, her heart forsook the Scriptures, and even now, I will cry over her. I sometimes wondered if she really had been saved. Maybe, just maybe, the Holy Spirit had found its way into her locked soul. However, was it my place to question his knowing? Part of me longed to know, but the other half wished to keep it a secret forever.

It was here I could escape my worries. Outside of this magical place, the world held me tight like a prison. I longed for the day I would be set free. But until then, I would come here. I would come here and soak in the

Father's comfort and love. Prayer would spring to my lips in this place, and songs of praise would over-take my heart and mind. My fears would dissolve quickly in the Lord's presence, like a single cube of dirty ice melting in a sparkling, clear lake.

Today I had come to escape the torturous life with my screaming aunt and her shouting husband, who were trying to get a divorce. My father was still in jail, and my older sister, who had not accepted the peace of God, was out on one of her dates. Only heaven knew where my brother was. He had run away for the eleventh time three days ago. Aunty had six children of her own, as well as the three children of her sister, my mother. All of them were at a friend's house except for Julie and two of the little ones, so I was unneeded.

My kneeling position shows that I was praying, and fervently. I never stopped praying for my family and I never have. My prayers were all different, but here is something like they used to sound:

"Dear Jesus,

I will start with my brother. He has a chance with You, Lord. I know he can make it. His heart is that of stone, but stone lasts not forever. Send his guardian angel with him in the darkest places he goes, and everywhere else as well. Let his blind eyes see the light, his deaf ears hear the truth, and keep him safe, wherever it is he dwells...

Now, Lord, I pray for my sister. She is a sinful child, but so was I, and so I am. The world is full of sinners, and your kingdom with cleansed trespassers. Let her conscience guide her in her relationships, and more importantly Your Spirit. Help her decide not to do things she will regret, and forgive her if she has already done those things....

Lord, you know of my father, as well as the things he has done. Forgive him, Lord. Help him forgive himself, and those who influenced him into wrong. Let this time in prison give knowledge to his mind, and humility to his heart. Help him see he cannot free himself, but will only dig himself deeper....

Jesus, I now pray for Aunty. Help her with her choice of friends and influences, as well as her future relationships. Help Julie, Joey, Helen, and I help her as much as possible. I pray for my cousins as well, that they would find you....

In closing, Lord, I pray for myself, that the daily bread still will find its way to my doorstep, that You will help me with my temptations and desires, and help me not procrastinate my visit to my father....

In Jesus name. Amen.

Eventually, I arose and reluctantly left the chapel, plucking my Bible off the ground. I stepped lightly down the gray steps, and into the still courtyard. The maple trees that were dotted here and there had already changed their colors to fall reds, oranges, and yellows. The grass had also yellowed from the coming autumn. I shivered once as the wind quickly rushed by. My blue sweatshirt was hardly enough to keep me warm, but it was the best I had, and I was thankful for it.

My old tennis shoes squeaked mildly as I ran down the stone path. I glanced down at them and vaguely noticed the huge holes at the knee-point of my jeans. Suddenly, something bright caught my eye, and I halted abruptly. I was staring down at a maple leaf. It was perfect, no cracks, or shredded parts. Wild yellow colored the outer edges, and then swirled into orange, then red at the center. Thin, yellow veins crisscrossed the intricate colors. The leaf reminded me of a fire. It was restless, blowing with the wind, and its colors fit the description.

Loud thundering interrupted my study of the leaf and I looked up. Dark clouds lined the top of the trees ahead of me, and lightning coursed from place to place. I reflected on my life, oblivious to the turmoil around me. Leaves gathered and swirled in nervous circles, and wind whipped my hair from my face, and ruffled the pages of my Bible. Only the bright leaf caught my eye as it flew away, its journey beginning right beside me. It twirled a few times, and then disappeared from my sight forever.

Big, fat drops of water began to fall, dotting the stone like a speckled gravel path. It was strange. A storm whirled around me, yet I was calm. My life raged like a storm, yet here I was, standing hand in hand with my Maker, and I was peaceful. I slowly pivoted to get one last look at my special place. Hectic maples and frantic ash trees surrounded the roofless church. It really was a magical place; a magical place that, along with my Rock and my Salvation, had shown me peace in my storm.

Award of Merit - 7th and 8th Grade Category

Jacob Wilson

8th Grade, Home Schooled

It Was Magical

We all know that Christmas is the most magical time of the year. Right? I think it is. It even smells magical, with the crisp, frigid nip of the air mixed with leftover wafts of cider and hot chocolate from Christmas parties come and gone. However, the most magical Christmas was back in 2007, and it certainly was one to remember.

It was the day before Christmas, Christmas Eve, and you could feel the excitement pulsating throughout the house. Over the radio, familiar holiday tunes lightened the atmosphere, and that patented Christmas smell drifted through the house. We had all day to kill playing indoors and wishing it was tomorrow. We had already sent in our Christmas lists to the head honcho of happiness (after we had gone through at least ten pieces of paper each remaking them), got all the decorations up, hung the stockings, put up the tree, vacuumed, packaged and sent our gifts to the relatives, and had run our supply of holiday movies completely dry. Even the T.V. didn't have a show we hadn't seen. As we were sitting there thinking of something to do, our weather alert went off in our utility room. We all scrambled past each other to get to it first (this was a little game of ours). I got to it just as it was saying that a severe flash flood watch was in effect. That sure did excite everyone. Not five minutes after we had heard the news, rain started its monotonous staccato on the roof of our house, and the rumbling echo of thunder rolled through the sky.

Another agonizingly slow hour crawled by before it was time for bed. We leapt into our beds and threw the covers over ourselves, and like every other Christmas, we couldn't go to sleep. I read a book, but mostly listened to the ever-increasing patter of rain falling in sheets against the side of the house. I eventually fell asleep, with visions of sugarplums dancing in my head.

I woke up before my brothers and shook them awake. We all left my room and walked into the kitchen, where my mom was sipping coffee. We were jumping up and down with excitement as we entered the piano room where our tree was. I recall myself tripping on my blanket I had wrapped around myself. Gift-wrap flew as we ripped open the packages, getting everywhere, even in my blanket. You can imagine what it was like.

After all our presents had been opened, I happened to glance out the window. All I saw was white everywhere. I ran outside with my blanket still wrapped about me and took in all the wonder around me. Everything had iced over. It seldom ices over where we live. Even the trampoline had iced over, sagging beneath the immense weight of many layers of ice. It was a complete Christmas. That was the most magical time ever.

First Place - 5th and 6th Grade Category

Lyndi Tsering

5th Grade, Home Schooled

The Eagle's Message

The sun was shining brightly through the loft window. Amy sat up in bed and shook her twin sister, Sara, awake. The girls were ten and had long blonde hair, cheery green eyes and a splash of freckles across their noses. Last summer, in 1875, Papa had moved them all out to this homestead on the prairie. Now they had gotten their claim for good and had a nice little cabin with a loft, where the girls slept, and two rooms downstairs.

Amy and Sara quickly put on their calico dresses and ran to the table. Sara's dress was sky blue and Amy's was lavender.

"Good morning girls! Did you both sleep well?" Mama said while dishing eggs onto everyone's plates.

"Yes!" the girls replied in unison.

Just then, Papa came in from feeding the animals. After he washed up, they all sat at the table and said grace. For breakfast, they had fried eggs, fresh biscuits, and bacon.

They had just finished when Jacob, their baby brother, started to howl. "Please go do the dishes, girls!" Mama hollered above the noise.

"Yes ma-am!" they shouted back and immediately ran to the corner where they hoisted up the tub between them to fill with water at the well. They walked out to the well where Sara held the bucket while Amy filled it with water. Amy was almost done filling the bucket with water when Sara grabbed her arm.

Three Wichita braves were walking toward them! The girls froze with terror. The braves picked up the girls and started off. Amy and Sara screamed, but it was no use; no one could hear them over Jacob's crying. They traveled like that for some time. The girls were terrified! What were they going to do? Would they ever see their family again? They were both silent with fear until much later when they reached the Wichita village.

Everyone stopped what he was doing and came to look at the girls. Amy shot a glance at Sara that said I don't like the way everyone is staring at us.

"Sakita!" One of the braves called. An old woman stepped out of the crowd and led the girls to her house. It was a strange-looking grass dome. Sakita had a well-decorated dress and big black circles painted around her eyes like a raccoon. She led the girls into the grass hut. There was an opening in the dome's ceiling. Smoke from a fire in the center of the hut billowed up and out the opening. Sakita sat down and motioned for the girls to sit, too. She painted black circles around their eyes and helped them into beaded dresses.

The girls helped her cook over the fire. Sakita sent them to pick berries. "I'm scared. How can we get back home?" Sara asked.

"I don't know what to do!" Amy said.

They had a nice supper of berries and unusual bread (which they decided was quite good) and then went to bed.

"Sara, are you awake!" Amy whispered. "Yeah, I can't sleep after all that has happened today, even though I'm really tired." Sara replied.

"Did you notice the strange pendant the chief wore with the eagle on it?" Amy asked.

"Yes, it was rather odd." Sara said sleepily.

"It gave me a funny feeling," Amy said. After a pause she added, "It was probably nothing." Then both girls rolled over and fell asleep.

Amy had just dozed off when she had a strange dream. *She was cooking over the fire when the chief passed by. Suddenly, the eagle from his pendant flew off and scooped Amy up, swooping through the sky with her and putting her down at her cabin door. Only a few seconds later he brought Sara to join her. Before they had a chance to thank him, he had vanished!*

Amy woke with a start the next morning. After breakfast, while they were picking berries again, Amy told Sara about her strange dream. "My dream was wonderful!" she exclaimed. "It was so… so… magical! I wonder if it was a message to us. Maybe the eagle can help!"

"I sure hope someone will," Sara replied.

Nothing unusual happened over the next two weeks. Both girls were anxious to see if anything would happen. Would the eagle really fly them home? Or would the pendant have a secret message? Their days were filled with cooking, berry picking, and sewing intricate bags. The work was so different from their normal chores that they almost enjoyed it.

"Do you think anything will happen? Maybe your dream was just a coincidence," Sara suggested.

"No, I'm sure it meant something," Amy insisted. And she was right.

Right after Amy fell asleep, she had another dream. *She and Sara were out washing their faces in the stream when the chief walked nearby to talk to his son. The eagle flew to them off the chief's pendant. He stared at Amy with a look as if he could tell what she was thinking.*

"Today is the day," he whispered. "Meet me at the stream." Then he flew off into the pendant and once more became lifeless.

Amy woke up, shaking with excitement. After breakfast while they were alone tending the fire, Amy told Sara about her dream. "We need to get to the stream with food and our other dresses. We'll need to bring the basket we use for berry picking."

They hastily collected food into the basket. They rolled up their dresses and hid them in the bottom of their basket. Would everything be all right? It was time to go. They looked at Sakita outside with another woman for the last time. Then they headed for the creek.

"Now what do we do?" Sara said.

"I'm not sure what to… look! It's the eagle from my dreams!" Amy said excitedly.

"I don't see an eagle," Sara stated.

"You have to trust me. Come on, he's ready to go!" Amy said impatiently.

"All right, if you're sure," Sara agreed uncertainly. The eagle began to fly slowly close to the ground.

All day the girls walked, Amy followed the eagle and Sara followed Amy. When they stopped to eat some berries and bread, the eagle silently waited for them on the ground. It was a long, hard, walk under the scorching sun, but the eagle never failed, although he did slow down when Amy and Sara grew tired. It was getting dark.

"Do you think we'll ever get home?" Sara asked.

"Of course we will!" Amy said cheerfully, though she was beginning to wonder herself. Just then, they saw their cabin up ahead. The twins ran all the way home, the eagle right ahead of them.

The girls burst into the house. "Amy, Sara, you're home!" They had a joyous reunion! Mama and Papa hugged them, kissed them, and hugged and kissed them again.

Amy turned around to the eagle just in time to see him vanish. "Thank you," she whispered. She was sure she saw a little sparkle in the air heading back to the Wichita village.

They told their story, talking late into the night. When they were too tired to say anymore, they took baths and put on fresh nightgowns. That night after Sara had fallen asleep; Amy went to the window and looked at the stars. She would never forget the eagle's message.

Award of Merit - 5th and 6th Grade Category

Brandon Grinovich

5th Grade, Home Schooled

A Day with a Super Hero

It was just an ordinary day for Duke Dimitri. He was out of bed at 9:00 a.m. and watching the latest episode of Superman. It was July 27th in the outskirts of Metropolis. Duke had devoured a delicious meal of fried sausage and scrambled eggs and was watching his favorite superhero pound and crush Lex Luther, one of Superman's worst enemies. As the credits rolled, Duke wondered, "Will I ever meet Superman?" What Duke did not know was that at that moment, the one and only Superman was headed for the house of Duke Dimitri.

Knock! Knock! Knock! "I'm coming!" bellowed Duke. As he opened the door, he almost passed out.

"Superman!" Duke exclaimed.

"Yes, it is me. Duke, I need you."

Duke could hardly believe his ears.

"Some of my worst enemies have formed an alliance and plan to destroy me," said Superman. "Will you be my sidekick?"

"Yes, I will!"

Duke, now equipped with laser guns and other cool gadgets, was headed to downtown Metropolis in Superman's car. Superman's enemies were coming into view. They had no idea what was about to hit them.

Duke was struck with fear, but only for a minute. He looked over at Superman and thought, "I'm safe."

Then, Superman hit the eject button on the dashboard and they went flying out the top of the car. Duke drew his laser gun and shot down two of the enemies. Duke and Superman landed and things got crazy. There were laser gunshots, battle cries, and screams of pain. The battle lasted for about an hour.

As the smoke and dust settled, there stood Duke and Superman. They were bruised and bleeding, but glad that some of Superman's enemies would not give him any more trouble. Duke went home bandaged and holding icepacks on his head and arm. However, he was overwhelmed with joy and wondered if he would ever have the privilege of helping Superman again.

kara Capps

Award of Merit - 5th and 6th Grade Category

Kara Capps

5th Grade, Home Schooled

Misty and Mystery: A Story of True Friendship

(Fiction)

Once upon a time in Trixie Land, it was a perfect day; the sun was shining, fairies of all kinds worked and whistled, everything was perfect except for – "Me."

With her head down, Summer Mist flew across the valley in which Trixie Land lay. She was a Light Fairy. People called her Misty if they did call her anything. She had a yellow-petaled dress with blond hair. Her hair was pinned up with a clip. Her lip trembled.

Misty stopped at a flower and sat down on it. Her wings drooped. She looked around as all the other fairies worked happily. They all had friends or pets. However, something was wrong. She had no one to work with. "If I had a friend... If I had a pet... If I were better at working, maybe I would get a friend...." Misty cried.

"Oh, Misty Twisty," a dark-haired fairy with pants and a black shirt said as she approached her. "I understand, Hunny Bunny."

"How?" Misty muttered. "You have lots of friends, Lillie, like Lissy and Jewel."

"Oh, sweetie pie," Lillie interrupted. "Of course you don't have any friends, you need to work harder!"

"You don't understand." Misty said feeling down.

"Well," said Lillie. "If you wouldn't sit around and do nothing and work more, maybe you'd get a friend."

"Lillie, just, just, leave me.... You don't understand and you'll never understand my life."

"Of course I do, Cup..."

"Cake," Misty said.

"I know about your ..."

Misty straightened her wings and swerved in the sky. "Of course I do, Cup Cake," Misty muttered copying Lillie.

She zigzagged through Trixie Land. As she got out of Trixie Land, she fluttered through a hollow bamboo stick. Fairies were ½ an inch, so they could squeeze through the earthworm's hole.

She looked around at the thick trees surrounding her. A tear dropped out of her eye. "I'll never get a friend," she sighed. She kept flying until she got to the lagoon.

Mermaids danced in the water. Their hair was one of green, silver, purple, pink, orange, and all the other colors of the rainbow. Misty watched as a redheaded mermaid played coral ball with an orange haired mermaid.

Mermen watched the girls play. They were protecting the girls. A brown haired merman watched the red-head who had red nails and a red fin. All of the mermaids had their fin color as their hair.

Misty longed to have one of them as her friend. But friends wouldn't last forever; what she needed was a pet – any pet - a bug even. A dark shadow caught her eye. It was big like a dragon, with wings like a dragon. Suddenly the red-headed mermaid dived into the lagoon. The others did the same. With a shaking body, Misty looked around.

L-L-Lillie? She shook harder. Then she saw a dragon. It was red with fire breath.

"Help!" Misty took off flying at her fullest speed. She saw other digging fairies dig in the ground to let other fairies in. "HELP!" she yelled.

She flew with the dragon behind her for one and one-half miles. Her wings felt tired. Her heart skipped a beat. Then she saw something she had never seen before. It was a tiny horse fairy. The horse fairy was grey with white spots on its back. She was sorry for it. It neighed very loud. "Here."

Misty flew to it and gave it a boost. She jumped on its back before it took off. It neighed wildly. It seemed to say thank you. As soon as the dragon was out of sight, the horse fairy landed on a red and orange spotted mushroom.

Misty got off. "There there," she said soothingly. She touched the horse fairy's face. It calmed down and neighed.

"You got a home?" Misty asked it.

It neighed.

"Well now you do." Misty smiled. "I'm Misty, and I think I'll call you," she eyed the horse fairy. "Mystery."

Mystery neighed happily. Misty got on Mystery and took off. She knew that she finally had a friend. They zigzagged and fluttered. They flew through tunnels and caves.

As they came out of a cave, Misty heard Mystery's heart beating furiously and his loud panting. Misty jumped off Mystery. "You want a rest, don't you?"

Mystery neighed and nodded. Misty sat down and played with a stone. Her heart was light with gladness.

Mystery lay down and Misty used Mystery's stomach as a pillow. She hadn't noticed how tired she was! She looked at Mystery. He was asleep. She listened to his soft breathing. Misty closed her eyes, and soon fell into a deep, deep sleep.

Whistles filled Misty's ears. Her eyes popped open. It was dark… so dark. "Mystery?" Misty called nervously.

No answer.

"Come out!" Misty shouted. A big slithery sound filled the darkness. Misty backed away from the sound, but then she tripped over a jagged item. She was flat on her back when light filled the place. It was a cave. Water dripped from the ceiling. A rock was in front of her.

"Mystery?" Misty shivered. It was cold, and she was all wet. "Is that you?"

"No," said the voice. It sounded like a girl.

"Show yourself!" Misty ordered.

"Ok! Ok! As you wish!" Misty heard.

Misty's eyes got big as she heard footsteps approaching her. In front of her was a huge, pretty, but big dragon. She was Green – evergreen, with dark blue eyes.

"W-w-who are you?" Misty stammered.

"You talking to me?" asked the dragon.

Misty nodded.

"Oh. I'm Kira and you don't have to be scared of anything. I don't bite," she said with a wink. When she opened her eye, it wasn't dark blue anymore. It was silver.

"Yikes!" Misty shouted.

"What?" Kira asked.

"Your… your eye!" Misty answered.

Kira took out a green grapevine mirror. "Oh, yeah, that! It's just my eye color." She frowned.

"But you have one blue eye and one silver eye," Misty said.

"Oh," Kira said.

Misty changed the subject. "I have to find Mystery!" She fluttered her wings, but she wasn't going up. Misty looked at her wings. They were caked with mud. "My wings!"

"Hold on, little fairy," Kira interrupted. "What's wrong?"

"I have to find Mystery!" Misty said.

"No can do," Kira said.

Misty stopped panicking. "Why?"

"The master of the dragons took him."

Misty panicked. "WHY?"

"Dunno… don't care… how's that?" Kira shrugged.

Anger filled Misty's mind. Why didn't Kira care? Misty took off running through the cave.

"Where are you going?" Kira shouted.

"To find Mystery!" Misty yelled. *Not as if you care,* she added silently.

Misty ran through the darkness. Suddenly her chin met a hard rock wall. Her lip trembled as pain shot through her chin. Misty turned around in the damp humid cave. She wandered the cave's paths for hours. It was so dark and she was hot. Her legs felt like Jell-O. The only thing that kept her going was Mystery.

"I have to find Mystery." Her legs felt as if they would collapse. She swerved back and forth so her legs would keep going. Her eyes felt like they were going to die. She had them open, but she couldn't see anything in front of her, not even her hand. She imagined the time when she and Mystery first found each other because of the dragon. Misty had been glad that the dragon came. Now she wondered if it would have been better if they never met.

As Misty walked through the lonely paths along the wall, light lit up in front and beside her. She squinted. It was so bright after walking in the dark cave. Her eyes stung. She looked into the light, and there was a big brown oval shaped door. On the side of it, it said, **Beware, Enter if You Dare!**

Misty took a deep breath and opened the door. Scary carvings and big spider webs with huge head-sized spiders were on the wall. There was a staircase. Misty wondered if she should go up and risk the danger that might be there.

A big slam caught her attention. She looked around. The door had closed behind her! Misty took a big breath. She slowly walked up the stairs. It was darker than it had been before the door closed. Glowing red eyes looked at her. They blinked. The only thing that kept her going was Mystery.

When she didn't see any more glowing red eyes in the darkness, she decided which way to go. She entered a door. It was dark, too dark. She didn't know how long she had been there. Seconds, hours, days, no, she'd die because of the lack of water and food. She wandered toward the doors, for what seemed like forever.

She daydreamed about Mystery. Misty wished that she were with him. How would she survive? Would she starve to death? Would a vicious animal attack her to the end? Would she die from the lack of water? All Misty knew was that she had to find Mystery.

It was said that Trixie fairies as she was, could only stay without water for a day, and humans could stay without water for two.

"Mystery!" Misty yelled. Bats fluttered around her. When was the last time she talked? It was no use. She'd never find her way out. She sat down on the creaky floor and started to cry.

A soft animal voice answered her. "Who's there?" It answered with an animal sound. It wasn't mean; it was sweet.

Misty asked another question, but it didn't answer. Misty knew it must have been her imagination. She got up her courage and roamed the rooms again. As she was walking, Misty heard a creak, and before she knew it, she was flat on her face, below the floor. Her head was drowsy. Everything was spinning.

Misty looked up. Light lit the air. Diamonds, crystals, rubies, emeralds, jewels, pearls, everything you could think of. It was a magical sight! Beautiful, lovely, and wonderful! The room was huge, crystals and diamonds filling all of it. There must have been hundreds of rooms! Misty strolled through the rooms. It was way too beautiful for her to take anything. As she wandered around the crystals, a soft neigh caught her attention. Misty looked around. It was Mystery! He was just as he used to be.

"Mystery!" Misty yelled.

Mystery neighed.

Suddenly they heard a loud roar. A big Dragon stomped into the room. Mystery galloped off to one of the rooms.

Misty's heart skipped two beats.

"Help!" Her voice sounded squeaky.

Then Mystery came back for Misty. She was running.

Misty's mud-caked wings made it hard for her to run. Mystery made her get on. The dragon followed close behind.

Mystery flew slower and slower because of Misty's mud-caked wings. Misty jumped off and hid behind crystals that were jagged out of the floor while Mystery flew to another room.

She had to find a way to get that dragon away! Then she had a thought. Everybody knew that Dragons were afraid of tiny monsters! But how would she get a tiny monster? She looked at the big dragon, and she looked at herself. She looked again and again. But how? Maybe Mystery? Maybe her collection of stuffed monsters at home? Maybe? Maybe?

That's it! Me! I can be a little monster!

There were vines on the walls. Misty took some and wrapped it around herself. She wrapped it around her face so only her eyes were showing, and she wrapped it around her legs so you couldn't see the skin, she wrapped it around her body so you couldn't see her dress.

She ran toward the dragon where Mystery had led him. Misty ran through the huge palace of pearls and crystals. There were hallways full of rubies. Misty toured the rooms running wildly.

Please be all right, Mystery! She thought frantically as she ran through rooms and rooms of jewels.

Again, she wondered if it would have been better if she had never met Mystery. Her blue turquoise eyes showed fear. *What if I don't make it in time? What if the dragon chopped Mystery to bits?*

When Misty approached, the dragon lost interest in Mystery and looked at Misty. He gasped and flew up. It made a huge hole on the ceiling. Above the ceiling was the haunted place. The big hole filled in with new wood and crystals.

Misty was lucky that no dragons had been up there when she was searching. Or was there? Misty had seen his glowing red eyes! There had been dragons! But why didn't they get her? Oh well. At least they hadn't.

Misty heard hoof beats. They were soft, sounding wonderful. Mystery came toward her. Misty hugged him. She tore off her monster costume. Another roar lit up. "Not again!" Misty yelled. Misty brushed off her mud-caked wings and flew. Mystery flew with her.

"Distract him while I get on the vines!" Misty said.

Mystery nodded. Misty turned around and flew to the vines. She wrapped her arms, her legs, her face, her clothes, and her hair with the vines. She ran to the dragon. He started to get scared.

Suddenly Misty's disguise broke off. The dragon laughed with fire coming out of his mouth. He grabbed Misty. He squeezed her tight.

"Ahhh!" Misty screamed.

Mystery neighed wildly as the dragon flew away with Misty. Mystery flew faster than the wind.

The dragon clung to Misty. What would Misty do now? It was up to Mystery now. She heard a buzzing sound. She looked back, thinking it was a bee fairy, but it was Mystery. He bit the dragon's back. The dragon let out a roar of pain. He tried to smash the horse fairy, as you would try to smash a fly. Mystery flew on top of his head.

The dragon held his hand up to smash Mystery but Mystery slid down his nose. He bit the dragon's forehead and flew down to Misty. Then he bit the dragon's fingers and the dragon dropped Misty.

Misty's leg was in pain. Her wings were bent so she couldn't fly. She couldn't leave. The dragon roared angrily at Mystery and picked Misty back up.

"Help!" Misty yelled.

Mystery flew faster and faster around the dragon. The dragon tried to catch him, but Mystery was too fast. The dragon's head spun in circles. He spun around just as fast as Mystery, but his head was getting weak. He shook his head. He had had enough of this. He dropped Misty, made a hole in the roof, and flew away.

Misty weakly got up. She straightened her wings. Her legs felt like spaghetti. She weakly ran to Mystery. She threw her arms around him and started crying.

"Mystery!" Misty beamed. "You're my best friend!" It had been a magical friendship with Mystery. She knew the only thing that kept her going the whole time was Mystery, her best friend in the world!

Award of Merit - 5th and 6th Grade Category

Jacqueline Madden

5th Grade, McCoy Elementary

Gold Cup

"Focus, Ivan, focus," screamed CD. It was the soccer practice the day before the minor gold cup. CD, their coach, stood for Coach Danver. He had hated Ivan, but Ivan loved soccer so he stuck it out. CD was boring; all they have been doing for two hours was passing in lines.

Practice had about two minutes before it was over. CD called everyone into a huddle. "Okay guys, the people that will be in the lineup for the first game are Chad, Aaron,

Will, Bryon, Alex, Carter, Ben, and Mike. Everyone has practiced their positions, so we can win a gold cup."

The entire team cheered except Ivan. "Um, CD," Ivan mumbled. "Am I in the line up anywhere?"

"No, practice is over, go home," said CD.

After the practice, Ivan's dad said, "Come on champ, cheer up."

"Why should I, I'm not going to play this whole tournament," said Ivan.

"Maybe you'll be the goal keeper?" said Ivan's dad.

"Um no, we have a goal keeper and he's not me!"

When the two of them got to the house, Ivan slammed the car door. He grabbed his soccer ball and marched upstairs. Ivan started to kick the ball at the wall.

"Want some dinner, super star?" called Ivan's dad.

Instead of responding, Ivan slapped the ball as hard as he could at the wall.

It was the morning of the first gold cup game, and instead of warming up with the team Ivan was sitting on the bench. He had a good team, and he was good as well, just not favored by CD.

Ivan watched all of the games from the bench, watching goal after goal, even all the gold cup games until the championship game. They were playing a good team, even better than they were.

It was the second half and it was 1-1. The big kid number 55 just pushed Mike, the best kid, on his ankle. The referee blew his whistle and CD ran onto the field and grabbed Mike.

"Ivan, you're on," yelled CD.

"What? What?" said Ivan.

"You're in... go... hurry... the clock is ticking," screamed CD.

Ivan ran onto the field. Alex had the ball and threw it down the line to Ivan. Once Ivan got a hold of the ball, he ran down the field and broke free.

He could start to feel the rain come down on his face. Ivan faked out the only defender standing on the goal box who had started to chase him. The opposition slipped in a mud puddle caused by the rain. Ivan sprinted to the goal. Their goalkeeper was standing there ready to go. Ivan propped his foot up, closed his eyes, and shot in the top left hand corner. He had done it!

The referee looked at his watch, and blew his whistle. Everyone ran up and hugged Ivan, and started cheering. Ivan felt a magical feeling inside, he felt like he was a champion.

1st Place – 4th Grade Category

Morgan Bishop

4th Grade, Ford Elementary

The Secret in the Closet

After school on Friday, I went over to my friend Samantha's house. She didn't go to my school, so she was probably at least a few minutes behind.

Ding-Dong. Her mom answered the door. She was wearing gloves, a red top, jeans, and muddy shoes.

"Hi, Mrs. Johnson. Have you been working in the garden?"

Yes," said Mrs. Johnson. "You can go upstairs into Samantha's room and wait for her."

I replied OK and went upstairs.

141

When I got to Samantha's room, I saw that the closet door was open and something inside caught my attention. I moved closer to see what it was.

AHAHAHAHAH! I fell into a deep, big, black hole. There was no sound until a small little voice broke the silence.

"Hi, I'm Perky."

"You're an elf," I screamed.

"Well, it took you long enough to notice. Anyway, let me show you around."

"This is our main street. It is the place where we elves do our shopping, sports, and our video games."

"Wow, do you know if Samantha knows about this world?" I questioned.

"Of course I do. She goes to school here," replied Perky.

That's impossible, I thought.

Perky interrupted my thinking and said, "Oh look, here comes my friend Penny."

"Hi Penny, I'm Hannah."

Does she know Samantha, I wondered aloud.

"Ha, Ha… of course I know her, she goes to my dance club. I see her every Tuesday when she gets out of school."

"Oh," Perky said. "I have to go now. I am due in an art club in a few minutes. See you later, Penny."

"Bye Perky. See you next time I visit."

"Oops, I forgot that I also have swimming lessons. See you later," Penny said.

All of a sudden, I was left alone in a strange place. Out in the distance, I thought I saw an elf boy. I wondered if this was all a dream and had fallen asleep on Samantha's bed, so I pinched myself. I knew this was definitely not a dream.

The boy approached me and said, "Hi, I'm Henry."

"Nice to meet you, my name is Hannah. Do you know my friend Samantha?"

"Of course I do," he replied. "She's in my music class. She sits in the third row directly behind me. One day Samantha played a neat song for us on the piano."

"I think she is in a dance club with an elf girl named Penny," I added. "Do you know Penny or Perky?"

"Yes," Henry replied.

"When is Samantha going to be coming back to her house?"

"Oh, about five minutes."

"Help, I have to get back to her house before she does."

I ran back to the black hole and tried to climb up the ladder. "Four steps left," I shouted to Henry. "Yes I made it. Bye, Henry. I'll see you next time I visit."

"See you later," yelled Henry.

When I got back to Samantha's house she was sitting on her bed watching T.V. I took a deep breath and told her the flat out truth. "I know about your elf world," I said quietly.

"YOU WHAT!" she yelled.

"I fell into the hole and discovered your secret."

She whispered to me and said, "You have to promise me that you won't tell anybody this, not even your mom."

"OK, I promise. By the way, your friends are very nice." I stood around the hole and yelled, "Goodbye. I will

145

visit all of you next time I come over, and I promise I will

keep your secret too!"

Award of Merit – 4th Grade Category

Catherine Dietlein

4th Grade, McCoy Elementary

My Step into the Future

"Mom, I'm home!" Creak. The door popped open. I peered inside. It was gray. The sad plain droopy gray walls we had moved into had remained tall and strong for all those years and were now all that was left. I wanted to break into tears but had to keep it together until I found out what really was going to happen.

"Oh, honey, you're home," my mom stammered. "Um... we're moving." She turned around and blew out so much air you'd think she said the world's longest tongue twister and made it through every single word.

I knew that tragic thought that was placed in my head was true.

She turned back around and coughed out, "I would appreciate it if you packed your things."

When my mom said the word "appreciate," it meant you had better do it.

I shuffled across the soggy halls to my room, which I would never see for the rest of my pointless life, sank into my pillow, and sobbed louder than a firecracker. I pulled myself together and trotted over to my closet, selected my feather slippers and chunked them into the box. Next, I picked up a photo of my mom and dad. I sighed as I noticed the date. It was two years before my dad died.

Just as I was about to shed another million tears, I spotted something glowing in the very back of my closet. I reached back and pulled out a necklace. It was just a rusty old chain with one single gem. On the gem an engraving read, "This will open many doors when you need them the most."

I was about to throw it behind my head, but a single ray of sunlight shown through the gem and a keyhole appeared on the wall.

All of a sudden, I noticed the gem was the same shape as the key hole. I blinked twice, but I wasn't dreaming. I put the gem in the lock, turned the doorknob and then the door opened. I stepped inside and shut the door behind me. This was not my house. There were happy colors all over this house. The only color left in my house was gray. I tried to open the door and go back into my room, but it was locked.

I took time to carefully study the room that I was in before I began to panic. There was a picture of me on the bookshelf with a smile on my face, standing next to a man. How could I be so happy with a strange man?

I glanced at the door and noticed a door hanger that read, "Cally's room....KEEP OUT!" The date on the door hanger read December 3, 2012. Today's date was January 13, 2009, and my name is Cally. So the only question I had was who is that man?

"Oh....sweetie you're home," my mom's voice echoed from the hall.

"Hi Cal," said the strange man patting me on the back. He seemed nice and I actually felt happy around him, but yet, I still wondered who he was.

"Oh honey, you know Robert. We got married two months ago," said my mom. I wanted to punch the air with excitement, especially because she married Robert, but I kept my cool.

"Honey, you are not yourself today. You're usually so happy all the time with Robert," said my mom in a surprised way.

This time I couldn't help but laugh aloud. No wonder I was so happy with him in that picture.

Then my smile faded as a thought grew in my head. "One question, mom," I said.

"Sure darling," my mom replied.

"Did we move?" I asked.

"Of course we did, darling. Did a coconut hit you on the head?" asked my mom with a puzzled look on her face. "We moved three years ago."

"Exactly where is here," I asked trying to get as much information as possible.

"You really need a nap," said my mom.

"I'm okay, mom," I said feeling faint. If this is the future, I can change it. Therefore, I had better be careful, because right now my future rests in my hands.

I felt a tingle in my fist. As I opened my hand, there sat the necklace. Looking at the engraving on the gem, I realized there was something special about it. I lifted it up to the sunlight to see it better, but then a single ray of sunlight shown through the gem and a keyhole appeared on the wall. I opened the door to see my mom standing there.

"I thought I told you to pack your things," she said annoyed.

"But you said you would appreciate it," I replied.

Book Magic

What is magical to you? I love books; books are my magic. When I read them, I feel like I soak into the words. I would tell you all about my magical experience, but this is only the introduction. I won't spoil the details.

I lay there in bed reading my small book I wrote in First Grade taking nothing out of it. I mean, the words are spelled wrong and out of place. I give up. This book is dumb. I threw my book on the hard floor and fell asleep.

I woke up the next morning and didn't hear the alarm clock go off or my mom calling, "Alexis get up." Instead, I smelt smoke and I was lying in bed with a huge dress on. Everything was pink. I hate pink. I panicked, as you always should when you don't know where you are.

I was still daunted as a little girl came in. I was wondering what would happen next. I stood there and watched her as it dawned on me I was in my pitiful little book I wrote in First Grade. I had a blank mind, knowing what would happen next. I came to the point where I was positive I was right.

I was prepared. I grabbed the little girl who was apparently my servant, grabbed my big pink mirror to use as a tool, and was ready to fight the dragon. The fierce fiery Dragon burst in with horror. He was right up in my face. It was Jurassic-sized; his teeth were as big as my head.

Throwing the mirror down on him was a mistake. The dragon was different from in my story. He was pleasant and calm. I liked him a lot. He lifted the girl and me carefully onto his green scaly back.

We rode through a coal-colored tunnel and in and out through many doors in a mystical castle. We rode through a dark forest and a light, fluffy, and wispy cloud. We finally stopped at a familiar sight, my home.

Of course, I missed my parents and friends, but I could not bear to leave the dragon and my new servant girl. I thought about my life back home and encouraged myself to get off the dragon's back. I could hop into this book anytime I wanted. Right?

With his wide wing, he dropped me down the chimney. Only after that, I remembered closing the wonderful story I wrote in First Grade and hearing my alarm go off.

This magical experience taught me you don't have to go anywhere to have a magical adventure. That misspelled book is now my dearest possession. Join my journey with me and read a good book.

1st Place – 3th Grade Category

Linden Carter

3rd Grade, Ford Elementary

Violin Amazement

If you ask me, I've never liked the violin. In some earlier part of my life, I wanted to play. But now? No. The worst part was in a few days, I was going to have a concert.

Anyway, I have a terrible teacher who is very strict and loves to give out homework. Today, he gave me a lot of homework. You may not think so, but that is your decision. My assignment was to practice the song Minuet three times a day for the concert. I agreed because no one wants to argue with him.

Day after day, my mom would ask me to practice, but I never wanted to and I knew there was no reason to whine. It felt as if days were minutes. Before long, it was Saturday, the day of the concert.

As I was walking in the performing area, I was trying to remember all the notes I was supposed to play. I was about to play the famous Minuet by Mozart. To me, that song was long, complicated, and had to be played fast.

Before I knew it, I was standing in front of the crowd. I told them my name, age, song, and who wrote the song. I lifted my violin onto my shoulder and started.

I wanted to close my eyes for the first few seconds and realized it was almost as if I was at home practicing without messing up. Also, it felt like my bow and my own hands were being controlled.

Every once in a while I would look up and see that everyone had their attention on me. The sound I was making sounded crisp, not squeaky; it was like the phrase "music to my ears."

After I finished, everyone clapped loudly. I felt so amazed and proud.

I now actually like the violin. I can't wait until my next concert!

Award of Merit – 3th Grade Category

Mary Pierce

3th Grade, Ford Elementary

A Magical Day

One morning there was a little girl named Caroline. She was thirteen years old. When she was a little girl, she wanted to be a fairy princess. Her mother said she would buy her a fairy every night after she had a spelling test.

When she turned thirteen, she wished for something that came true. The next morning she looked up in the mirror and said, "Mom!"

"Yes, Honey."

"What has happened to my face and my… my body?"

"Well, Honey, it's at least what you have always wanted to be."

"Hey, you're right. I shouldn't worry. OK, then where's my carriage?

"Well, first you are going to have to go on an adventure."

"An adventure? Now I know I have wings, but I have not even learned how to fly."

"I will teach you how. You don't know how to fly. I do. When I was your age I wished something and it came true."

"What was the wish?"

"I wished that I could be a fairy princess. It came true. However, I didn't like fairies as much as you did, so I got tired of it. On my sixteenth birthday, I wished that I were not a fairy anymore. So the next morning I was just a normal person."

"Wow. Were you sad?"

"Ummm, not really. I was a little bummed because I heard that my mother and father died in a car crash. I was sent to an orphanage. Soon, a lady adopted me."

"What was her name?"

"Sylvie."

"Did you call her by her first name?"

"Yes. We need to get back on track."

"Okay, where do we need to go?"

"We?"

"Caroline, you have to do it on your own."

"Why?"

"It happened to you."

"Well, can you at least teach me how to fly?"

After the practice was over, off Caroline went. While she was flying, she saw another fairy.

"Hello," said Caroline. "What's our name?"

"Sara. What's yours?"

"Caroline."

"I like that name."

"Thanks. Where are you going?" asked Caroline.

"I am going to do an adventure to see where the other fairies are."

"Me too. Maybe we can do it together."

"That would be a great idea. Which way do we go?

"Let's go down fairy path."

While they were walking, they saw houses. Not just ordinary houses, there were houses with flowers covering them. Some had fairy dust, even candy. It's like a gingerbread fairy house, instead of a gingerbread house. "I wish I could have one," said Caroline.

"Me too. Hey, how about we go ask that lady at the front desk?"

"Okay."

"Excuse me. Can we buy a house?"

"Well of course. What you do is you find a house with a For Sale sign on it. Go in the house. Look around. If you like it then look at the price and make sure it's okay with you. Come back to me. I will give you a key. Then I will give you two hundred bucks to spend at the store," the lady at the front desk explained. "When you get to the store, find two beds, two dressers, one telephone, toiletries, and lots of clothes. Set up your house. There's already a full kitchen. I will buy you some food. Do not forget shoes."

"Okay, that's a lot of directions. We can do it. Let's start," Caroline said.

"Hey, that's a nice house. Let's go look inside."

"Okay. I like that house."

"Me too. The price is okay. Let's go get the key."

When they got the key and the money, they went shopping. After they were done shopping, they set up their house. They got their food.

The lady said, "I have one more surprise for you."

"Yes."

"It's… a car. It's called a buggie."

"Thank you, thank you."

"You're welcome. Good night."

"Good night."

The next morning they got up and did their daily routine, which is take a shower, brush their teeth, brush their hair, eat breakfast, and get dressed.

"Let's find a job. I want to be a veterinarian," said Caroline.

"I want to be a gymnast. Now let's find the places where we want to work."

"Hey, there's the gymnastic place. Hiring coaches. There's a sign that says, hiring coaches. Let's go sign you up."

Okay."

After Sara got a halftime job, they went to find Caroline's job. "There's a vet. It says, hiring dog trainers. Let's go sign up to get you a job."

"Okay."

After they got their jobs, they went to get a car. "I want a Chevy," Sara said.

"Okay."

After they got a car, they went to do their jobs. They went to a restaurant after they were done with their jobs. Then they went home.

The next day they went to buy a pet. They got fish, guinea pigs, rats, and three dogs. The guinea pigs' names were Cookie Dough and Shadow. The rats' names were Curios, Darling, and Nervous. They got so many fish they could not name them and they had to put them in two fish tanks.

"Do you want to call your mom first, or mine?" asked Caroline.

"You can go first."

She dialed the number, eight, six, nine, two, nine, two, three, and five. "Hi mom."

"Hi."

"I'm coming back tomorrow."

"Cool. I thought you would never come back."

"Me neither."

"Bye."

"Bye, honey."

"Oh no."

"What?"

"I forgot all about work. We better hurry."

After they went to work, they started to pack up. "Well, do you want to walk home together?"

"Where do you live?"

"Vista Oaks."

"What street?"

"Laurel Bay Loop."

"Me too!"

@Georgetown, Texas

4774097R0

Made in the USA
Charleston, SC
15 March 2010